EXAMINING DISASTERS

EXAMINING EARTHQUAKES

BY JACOB YANG

CLARA HOUSE BOOKS

First published in 2015 by Clara House Books, an imprint of
The Oliver Press, Inc.

Copyright © 2015 CBM LLC

Clara House Books
5707 West 36th Street
Minneapolis, MN 55416
USA

Editors: Mirella Miller and Arnold Ringstad
Series Designer: Maggie Villaume

All rights reserved.

Picture Credits
Shutterstock Images, cover, 1, 12, 37; U.S. Navy, 4; Gurgen Bakhshetsyan/Shutterstock Images, 7; Dorling Kindersley/Thinkstock, 9; The Yomiuri Shimbun/AP Images, 11; Boris Grdanoski/AP Images, 14; Richard Ward/Dorling Kindersley RF/Thinkstock, 17; Masanobu Nakatsukasa/The Yomiuri Shimbun/AP Images, 18; Enric Marti/AP Images, 21; Red Line Editorial, 22; USGS, 25; Thinkstock, 26, 34; AFLO/Nippon News/Corbis, 28–29; Binsar Bakkara/AP Images, 31; Library of Congress, 32; Jeremy Hogan/Bloomington Herald-Times/AP Images, 39; Dmitry Morgan/Shutterstock Images, 40–41

Every attempt has been made to clear copyright. Should there be any inadvertent omission, please apply to the publisher for rectification.

Library of Congress Cataloging-in-Publication Data

Yang, Jacob, 1974-
  Examining earthquakes / By Jacob Yang.
     pages cm – (Examining disasters)
  Audience: Grades 7 to 8.
  ISBN 978-1-934545-63-8 (hardcover : alk. paper)
 1. Earthquakes–Juvenile literature. I. Title. II. Series: Examining disasters.
  QE521.3.Y35 2015
  551.22–dc23
                                           2014044621

Printed in the United States of America
CG1022015

www.oliverpress.com

CONTENTS

CHAPTER 1
Catastrophe at Fukushima Daiichi
5

CHAPTER 2
What Is an Earthquake?
13

CHAPTER 3
How Earthquakes Happen
19

CHAPTER 4
Earthquake Effects
27

CHAPTER 5
Earthquake Safety
35

TOP TEN WORST EARTHQUAKES 44
GLOSSARY 46
FURTHER INFORMATION 47
INDEX 48

ONE

CATASTROPHE AT FUKUSHIMA DAIICHI

On March 11, 2011, things appeared normal at the Fukushima Daiichi Nuclear Power Plant in Fukushima, Japan. But deep underground, stress was building in Earth's crust. At 2:46 p.m. local time, a powerful earthquake struck 15 miles (24 km) below the surface of the Pacific Ocean. The earthquake occurred 78 miles (126 km) off the east coast of Japan and 111 miles (178 km) from the Fukushima Daiichi plant. The force of the earthquake made buildings rock and fires ignite 235 miles (380 km) away in Tokyo, Japan's capital. What became known as the Tohoku earthquake was felt as far as Beijing, China, which is more than 1,300 miles (2,090 km) away!

A city near the port of Sendai in Japan was washed away after the earthquake.

TSUNAMI PREPAREDNESS

Tsunamis are one of the deadliest natural disasters known to man, and earthquakes usually trigger them. The 2004 Indian Ocean earthquake and tsunami killed nearly 230,000 people. Effective warning systems are a key preparedness element. Sea walls can help break the force of a tsunami and can protect a city from the high waves. Sirens warn residents when a tsunami is coming. Then, residents can evacuate threatened areas for higher land. But tsunamis are likely to remain a destructive and deadly weather event, since there is not enough warning time.

Initial measurements put the quake at an 8.8 or 8.9 magnitude on the Richter scale, which seismologists use to measure the strength of an earthquake. These estimates were later changed to 9.0. On average, fewer than three earthquakes with a magnitude of 8.0 or greater happen each year. The Tohoku quake was the fourth strongest since 1900, and it was the worst quake ever to hit Japan. The earthquake also caused a tsunami with waves 45 feet (14 m) high at Fukushima. The tsunami destroyed buildings and swept away vehicles and crops.

The Fukushima Daiichi Nuclear Power Plant sat in the path of the tsunami. The power plant had sensors to warn it of earthquakes. These sensors activated, and as

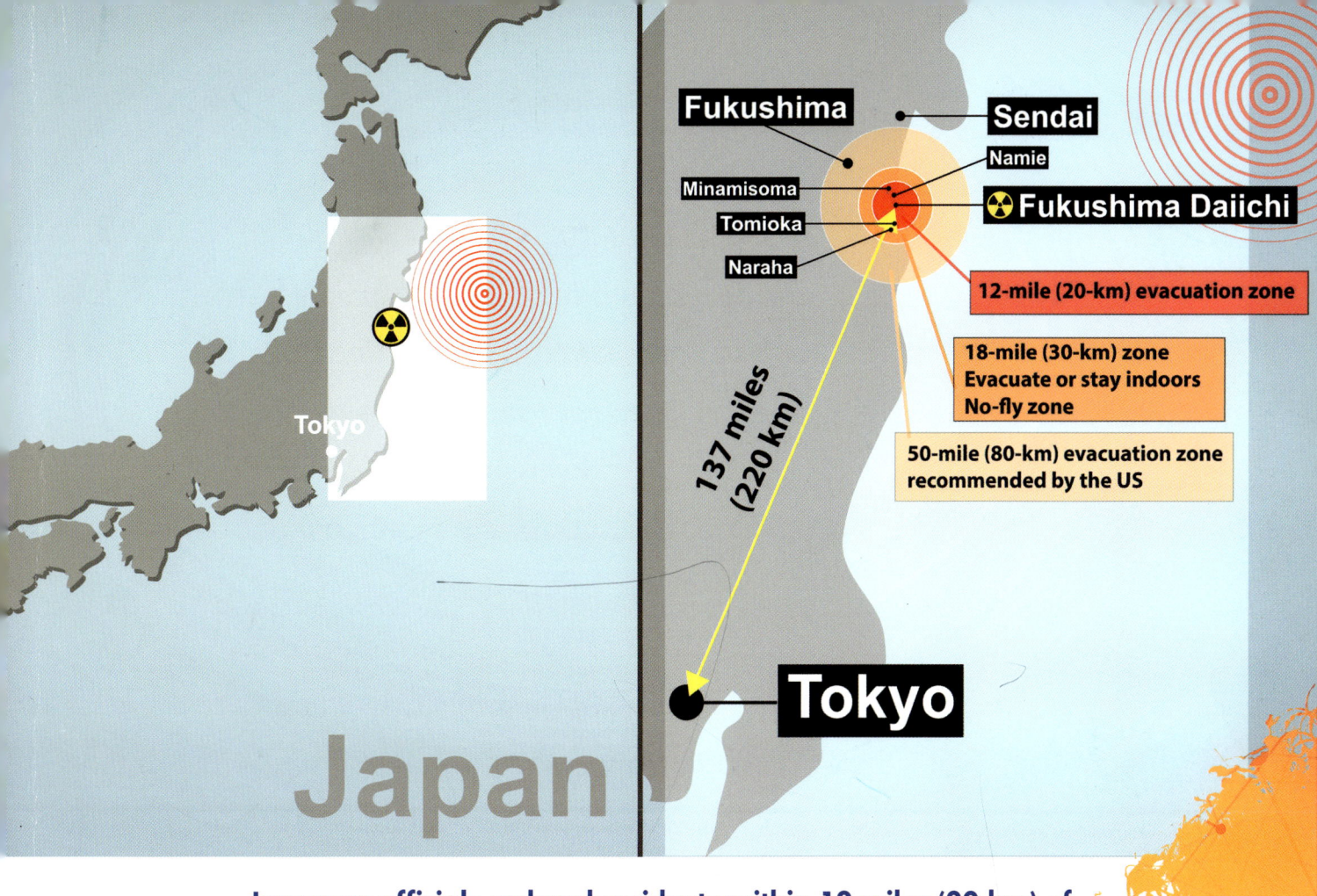

Japanese officials ordered residents within 12 miles (20 km) of the plant to evacuate because of radiation concerns.

a safety precaution the plant's reactors shut down. But three of the reactors were still hot and required cooling. If a nuclear reactor gets too hot, it can release harmful radiation into the atmosphere, in what is called a meltdown.

Fifty minutes after the earthquake struck, a 45-foot (14-m) tsunami rushed over the plant's sea wall. The plant was running on emergency diesel generators after the earthquake had knocked out its electrical power. But the tsunami wave knocked the generators out, too.

BELOW THE CRUST

Earth is made up of three major layers. The top layer is called the crust. The crust is the thinnest layer, averaging 25 miles (40 km) thick. The middle layer is called the mantle. Near the crust, the mantle is solid rock. As the mantle nears the inner core of the planet, it becomes so hot that the rock melts into liquid. The inner core is the extremely hot innermost layer. Scientists believe the solid core is made of the metals iron and nickel.

The plant had to rely on backup battery power to cool its reactors. The batteries ran out of power the following day, March 12. Without a power supply, the plant could not cool its reactors.

The pressure in the reactors built up quickly. Officials vented radioactive material into the air to prevent a larger, uncontrolled release. If too much pressure had built up inside the reactors, they could have burst and released even more radiation. The disaster displaced more than 100,000 people who had to live in temporary housing, stay with relatives, or move to different cities.

AFTERMATH OF THE TSUNAMI

On December 16, 2011, more than nine months after the tsunami hit Fukushima, Japanese Prime Minister Yoshihiko

THE LAYERS OF EARTH
This diagram shows the layers of Earth. After reading about the layers, what did you imagine they looked like? How does seeing this diagram help you understand how the crust relates to the rest of Earth's layers?

Noda announced the plant's reactors had finally been safely cooled and fully shut down.

The Tohoku earthquake changed the lives of thousands of Japanese people. The quake, tsunami, and nuclear accident left more than 19,000 people dead and more than 6,150 injured. More than 1 million homes were damaged or destroyed. Millions of Japanese citizens lost access to water, electricity, and food. Some Japanese citizens grew distrustful of nuclear power. Many called for the government to shut down nuclear plants.

A tsunami wave from the Pacific Ocean approaches coastal houses in Japan on March 11, 2011.

Around the world, scientists and citizens called for nuclear power plants to be inspected and improved. They wanted added safeguards against earthquakes to avoid a disaster like Japan's.

Seismologists rushed to Japan to study the Tohoku earthquake. They hoped to learn more about how and why earthquakes happen. Seismologists want to predict more accurately when and where the next earthquake will hit.

Large earthquakes can be terrifying events for the people they affect. They are powerful natural disasters. Strong earthquakes destroy towns and collapse buildings. They also create deadly seismic waves and reshape Earth.

TWO

WHAT IS AN EARTHQUAKE?

Unlike shaking caused by humans and machines, such as explosions or drilling, earthquakes cause shaking through the movement of tectonic plates along fault lines. Tectonic plates are a set of many drifting surfaces that make up Earth's crust. Fault lines occur and mountains can form at the borders between these plates. When plates move past each other at fault lines, earthquakes can happen.

An earthquake is often composed of several smaller quakes. Sometimes foreshocks, or smaller quakes, happen before the main earthquake. Scientists do not know at first whether a quake is a foreshock or a main quake. They wait to see if a larger earthquake follows.

A road is unusable in the aftermath of an earthquake.

Seismographs record earthquake vibrations as movements from a needle on paper.

Then they make observations and recordings. If a stronger earthquake follows within a certain time period, then scientists know the first quake was a foreshock.

Seismologists call the biggest quake the mainshock. It causes most of the damage. Mainshocks are almost always followed by smaller quakes, called aftershocks. Seismologists have observed that strong earthquakes have more aftershocks than mild earthquakes. Aftershocks often take place in the days following a mainshock, but can also happen months or years later.

Seismologists take measurements to figure out whether a quake is an aftershock, rather than a new earthquake. First, seismologists measure the rupture front.

SEAFLOOR MOVEMENT

The movement of the tectonic plates that brought about the 2011 Tohoku earthquake caused the seafloor to shift by 79 feet (24 m) east to west. Seismologists received this measurement from sensors they used to monitor the area. The seismologists tracked the location of their sensors after the earthquake, giving them a before-and-after picture of how far the seabed had moved. The ocean floor is now 100 feet (30 m) closer to Japan than it was before the earthquake.

The rupture front is the exact location where the tectonic plates overlapped. Seismologists measure from the spot where the slip started to the location where it stopped. This is called the rupture distance. Any earthquake that occurs within one or two rupture distances of the mainshock is classified as an aftershock.

MEASURING EARTHQUAKES

Seismometers are machines that record vibrations in the ground. Seismologists use them to detect earthquakes and

HOW SCIENCE WORKS
PREDICTING EARTHQUAKES

Seismologists, scientists who study earthquakes and plate tectonics, have created tools that detect earthquakes and send warnings out after an earthquake begins. But earthquakes move quickly, and warnings often do not come in time to save everyone.

Earthquake prediction is not very accurate. However, seismologists can identify fault lines and areas where earthquakes are more likely to occur over a certain period of time. Major fault lines occur where tectonic plates meet, but smaller and less active faults can occur anywhere there is a fracture or other deformity in the crust. Predictions are not as accurate as seismologists would like. Seismologists experiment to find better ways to predict earthquakes. They study earthquakes, looking for patterns. If they identify a pattern of when and where earthquakes happen, that pattern may help them predict where the next earthquake will strike. Then, they can warn communities ahead of time.

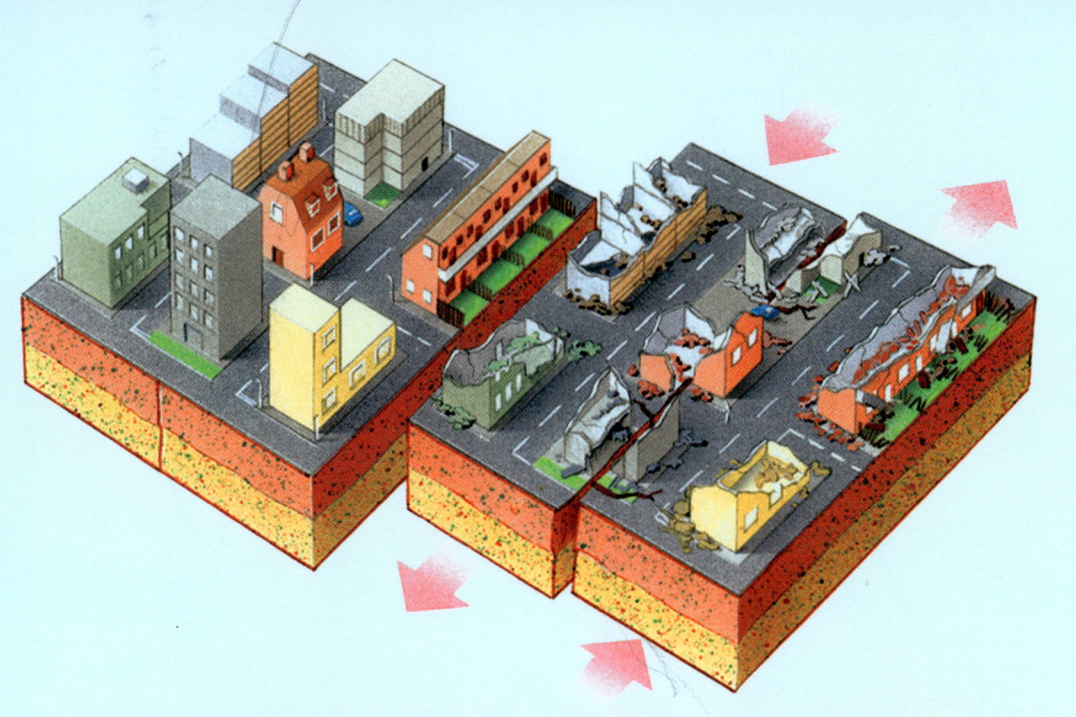

BEFORE AND AFTER
The diagram above shows a city before and after an earthquake. What has changed? What has stayed the same? What might be the reasons for the changes?

measure their power. Earthquake magnitude is reported and compared using two scales. The Richter scale works best for small earthquakes. Seismologist Charles Richter created this scale in 1935. The Richter scale measures the amplitude, or height, of the greatest seismic wave recorded on a seismometer. Although it ranges from 0 to 10, this scale is most accurate for earthquakes measuring 3.5 or less. The moment magnitude scale is more scientifically accurate. It measures the size of earthquakes, which is helpful in measuring larger earthquakes.

THREE

HOW EARTHQUAKES HAPPEN

The shifting of Earth's seven major tectonic plates and dozens of smaller plates causes earthquakes. Movement of the Pacific and North American plates against each other causes earthquakes in California. The plates move extremely slowly, forming new crust and grinding old rocks into sand and dust. The Pacific plate moves northwest, sliding under the Okhotsk plate beneath Japan at a rate of 3 to 4 inches (7 to 11 cm) per year. On the surface, the effects of this movement are most visible along fault lines.

The jagged plate edges cause the fault lines to be uneven. The uneven edges can get caught on each other, causing stress to build up below Earth's surface.

The movement of the Pacific plate against the Okhotsk plate caused the 2011 Tohoku earthquake.

Seismic waves can cause severe damage near an earthquake's epicenter.

THE MARIANA TRENCH

The deepest spot on Earth is the Mariana Trench. Its deepest spot is the Challenger Deep, which sits 36,201 feet (11,034 m) below the surface of the Pacific Ocean. The Mariana Trench sits on the border of two tectonic plates in a subduction zone. This is a place where one plate moves below another. Any earthquake originating from the subduction zone in the Mariana Trench could have a magnitude of approximately 8.5 on the Richter scale and cause widespread destruction.

When the stress becomes too great, the plates grind against each other or one plate pushes above the other. The location where the stress is finally released is called the hypocenter, which is where the earthquake starts. A wave of energy travels up to Earth's surface from the hypocenter. The spot on Earth's surface directly above the hypocenter is known as the epicenter.

The pressing, sliding, and grinding motion of the plates creates waves of energy called seismic waves. These waves ripple outward in all directions from the epicenter. They travel along the surface of Earth, causing the shaking of an earthquake.

P WAVES

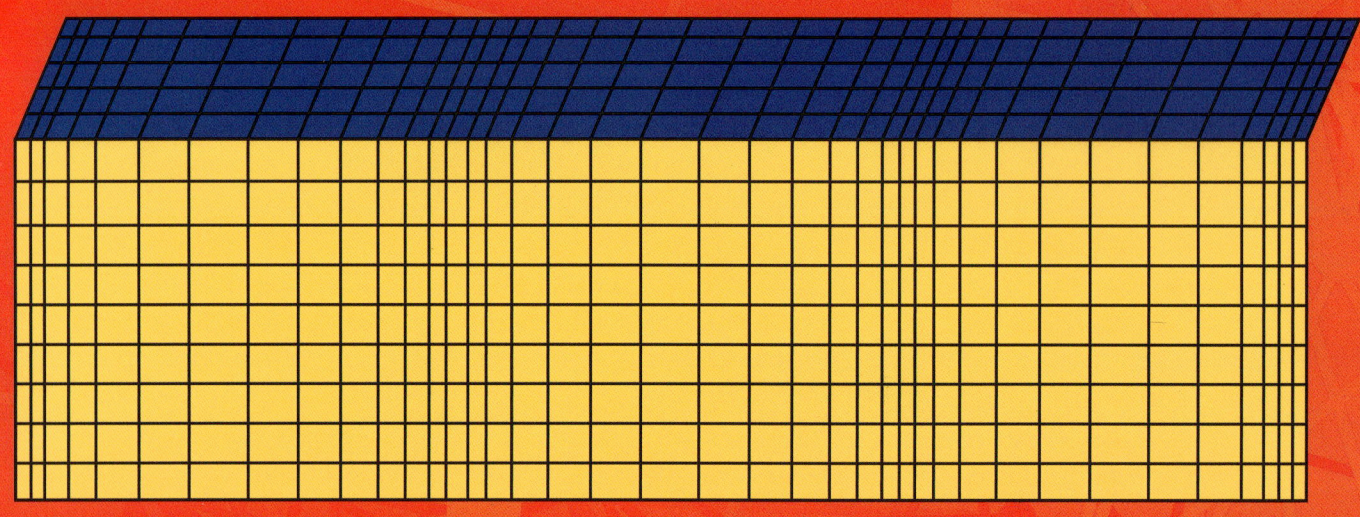

→ WAVES ARE TRAVELING THIS WAY

S WAVES

S waves travel more slowly than P waves, so people typically feel P waves first.

TYPES OF SEISMIC WAVES

During an earthquake, shaking causes damage in various ways. There are four main types of seismic waves, each with different effects. One kind, which shakes the ground from side to side, is called a P wave. P waves are also called compressional waves, because they compress and expand the ground like a spring.

Another kind of seismic wave is called an S wave. It shakes the ground up and down, and it causes an earthquake's rolling motion. P and S waves are both called body waves, because they travel within the ground.

The two other types of seismic waves are called surface waves. They move along Earth's crust, while body waves move through all of Earth's layers. Surface waves move slower than body waves and have a lower frequency.

EARTHQUAKES CAUSED BY HUMANS

The shifting of massive plates does not cause all earthquakes. Humans can cause some earthquakes. Injecting fluids into deep wells to extract petroleum and

Oilfield waste is injected into deep wells for permanent storage underground. This process can trigger earthquakes.

natural gas in a process called hydraulic fracturing, or fracking, has caused earthquakes. These earthquakes have been relatively minor so far. Humans have also caused earthquakes by exploding bombs underground, removing rock from mines, and creating reservoirs behind dams. These activities change or add to the tension on the surrounding rock. This change causes the rock to release its tension and shift into a position of less strain. This shift is an earthquake.

HOW SCIENCE WORKS
PLATE TECTONICS

Plate tectonics is the theory that Earth's crust is made up of large, slowly moving plates. One of the earliest suggestions that continents were not permanently fixed in their locations came in 1596. A mapmaker named Abraham Ortelius noticed the edges of the continents seemed to fit together. Centuries later, in 1912, German scientist Alfred Wegener had a similar idea. He believed Earth's continents had been joined as one supercontinent in the distant past. But other scientists rejected his idea, because Wegener had no explanation for how the continents had moved apart.

Scientists found evidence for Wegener's theory in the 1950s, as people mapped the seafloor. They discovered ocean ridges, underwater mountains that had formed where continents had likely moved apart. Like many scientific theories, plate tectonics was not widely accepted at first. But after decades of study returned large amounts of supporting evidence, scientists accepted the theory as the best explanation for the structure and movement of Earth's crust.

FOUR

EARTHQUAKE EFFECTS

Being in an earthquake can be terrifying. Without warning, the ground suddenly starts shaking under your feet. If you are outside, the quake could knock you to the ground. In a building, it might feel as though the structure will collapse. Items can fall from shelves or the ceiling. Even though earthquakes often last less than a minute, they can cause enormous amounts of damage. Earthquakes can cause buildings to collapse, roads to split apart, and unstable pieces of ground to break off, leading to landslides. In Peru in 1970, an earthquake caused a landslide that moved at the rate of 100 miles (160 km)

Powerful earthquakes can quickly reduce an entire neighborhood to rubble.

Tsunami waves can devastate towns and cities on coastlines.

per hour. It destroyed villages and killed more than 70,000 people.

The amount of damage an earthquake causes is related to where it strikes, particularly if it is in a populated area. If a quake happens far from a city, it may have little effect on people. But in populated areas, damage and danger can affect people greatly. Sometimes, the shaking damages structures directly.

Other times, damage occurs when the ground settles into a new position after the earthquake.

Along coastlines, earthquakes can cause damage from flooding. Shaking can break dams or levees, releasing water into streets and towns. A tsunami can form when the ocean floor shakes up and down. The tsunami wave grows larger as it moves, pulling water into itself. The giant wave rushes toward shore, flooding whatever is in its path.

This aerial view shows the damage caused by the magnitude 9.1 earthquake and tsunami near Sumatra, Indonesia.

2004 INDIAN OCEAN TSUNAMI

The 2004 Indian Ocean tsunami in South and Southeast Asia was one of the deadliest of all time. A magnitude 9.1 earthquake struck off the coast of the Indonesian island of Sumatra at 7:59 a.m. local time on December 26. The tsunami traveled and grew for seven hours, making landfall as far away as the east coast of Africa. The tsunami took its heaviest toll in Indonesia. The tsunami destroyed many roads and other structures, making it nearly impossible for aid to reach some areas. In addition to those killed during the tsunami, many people died over the following days and weeks because they lacked food, water, and medical attention.

Earthquakes can also cause a great deal of damage after the shaking is over, as was the case in the San Francisco earthquake

THE RING OF FIRE

Seismologists know 90 percent of the world's earthquakes happen along a seismically active belt called the Ring of Fire. This strip winds around the Pacific Ocean like a horseshoe, touching the coasts of North and South America, Japan, the Philippines, and the island nations north of Australia. Several tectonic plates collide along the Ring of Fire. The area is also known for frequent volcanic eruptions.

People look at the damage from the 1906 earthquake and fire in San Francisco.

of 1906. The earthquake caused underground water pipes to break. When fires started because of the earthquake, firefighters were unable to get water to put out the blazes that spread through the city. Engineers later designed water pipes that could survive an earthquake.

SUPERCONTINENTS

Tectonic plates move just a few inches each year, but over time those movements add up. More than

270 million years ago, most of the planet's landmasses were combined into a single supercontinent called Pangaea. Pangaea covered almost one-third of Earth's surface. Then, 200 million years ago, Pangaea began to break apart as the tectonic plates underneath the landmass shifted. Pangaea split apart over hundreds of millions of years, forming today's continents and oceans. The movements of the tectonic plates are bringing the continents together again. It has been estimated that in the next 50 million years, Africa, Australia, and Eurasia will combine to form a new supercontinent.

HOW SCIENCE WORKS
LIQUEFACTION

Liquefaction creates some of the most dangerous effects of earthquakes. It occurs when the shaking of Earth causes water in the ground to soak into surrounding soil. The soil begins to behave like a liquid, flowing instead of standing still and supporting structures above it. Without that ground support, buildings, roads, and underground pipes can collapse.

Seismologists and engineers work to prevent this kind of damage. Seismologists know some areas have greater risk of liquefaction. Seismologists use instruments to measure the soil. They drill deep into the earth to take samples to see how sandy and dense the soil is. The seismologists use their observations to tell engineers where it is safest to build.

FIVE

EARTHQUAKE SAFETY

Although they have learned much about earthquakes, seismologists are not yet able to predict when or where the next earthquake will be. As a result, earthquake safety focuses on earthquake preparedness rather than prediction. Seismologists make recommendations to governments, engineers, and citizens to help communities prepare for the effects of earthquakes.

One important safety step is a network of tsunami warning systems along coastlines. Governments construct these systems to alert communities if an earthquake has triggered a tsunami nearby. This gives people time to move to

Scientists set up equipment to measure earthquake effects, giving them a better idea of how earthquakes work.

Construction on the Bay Bridge in San Francisco will provide more stability for the bridge during future earthquakes.

RETROFITTING

One way to minimize an earthquake's damage is to retrofit structures so they are not destroyed. Structures built before the 1990s often must be strengthened so they can withstand an earthquake. Sturdy metal plates and beams are bolted onto the structure to anchor it to its foundation. These additions ensure the structure will not slide off its foundation during the shaking of an earthquake.

higher ground before the tsunami waves reach the shore.

Another important safety step is developing requirements that new roads and structures are strong enough to withstand an earthquake. Public buildings and bridges that existed before the new rules went into effect can be upgraded so they will survive an earthquake, too, in a process known as retrofitting.

ARCHITECTURE

Many different factors affect how well structures survive earthquakes. Building shape is one factor. Square or rectangular buildings are often more stable during earthquakes than structures with rounded shapes. Materials are another factor. Flexible materials, such as steel and aluminum, are better at withstanding earthquakes than brittle materials, such

> **If you find yourself in an earthquake, take cover under something sturdy, such as a table or desk.**

as brick and stone. Flexible materials can move with the forces created by earthquakes, rather than resisting the forces and breaking. Engineers must also pay attention to the kind of soil beneath buildings. If there is a risk of liquefaction, builders should construct a foundation designed to handle the shifting soil and prevent a collapse.

When comparing areas that have earthquake-ready building codes to areas without them, the difference in damage can be enormous. The 1994 Northridge earthquake in California had a magnitude of 6.7. It took place in densely populated Southern California, but building regulations in the area were designed to protect against earthquakes. Sixty people died. Nine years later, a magnitude 6.6 earthquake hit Bam, Iran. The area did not have earthquake-ready building codes, and more than 30,000 people died. Careful engineering is the first step in preventing earthquake damage.

SAFETY STEPS

Families can also take steps to prepare for earthquakes. If water pipes and power lines are damaged in a quake, a

Even though it is not known when earthquakes will happen, it is important to be prepared and stay safe.

family may be left without clean water and electricity. The Federal Emergency Management Agency recommends that families living in earthquake-prone areas always keep enough food, water, and other supplies on hand to last 72 hours after an earthquake.

Another major danger of earthquakes comes from falling objects that are knocked loose by shaking.

To prevent injuries, families can fasten shelves securely to walls and hang heavy items, such as picture frames, away from couches or beds.

Knowing what to expect and what to do during an earthquake can keep you and your family safe. If you feel an earthquake, drop to the ground so you do not fall down. If you cannot find shelter under something strong, move to a corner and cover your head and face with

SHAANXI PROVINCE EARTHQUAKE

The deadliest earthquake ever recorded struck Shaanxi, China, in 1556. The estimated magnitude 8 quake killed or injured approximately 830,000 people. According to records from the time, the earthquake lasted only a few seconds, but it leveled mountains, altered the course of rivers, and caused widespread destruction. After the quake, survivors replaced the destroyed stone buildings with those made of more flexible materials, such as bamboo and wood. The inhabitants of Shaanxi were some of the first to adapt their architecture to protect against earthquakes.

your arms. If you are outside, move away from buildings and power lines.

Earthquakes are powerful forces of nature. Like the Tohoku earthquake, they can be destructive. Seismologists hope that by studying how and why earthquakes happen, they will become better at predicting where and when the next one will hit. Perhaps some day, seismologists will be able to predict earthquakes. Until then, people must follow safety precautions to reduce the danger from these deadly disasters.

CASE STUDY

THE SAN FRANCISCO EARTHQUAKE OF 1906

On April 18, 1906, near San Francisco, California, movement occurred at the boundary between plates, causing a huge earthquake. At that time, scientists did not know what caused earthquakes. Scientists all over California took photographs, drew pictures, and wrote detailed notes. They realized the worst damage was close to the fault line.

Today, seismologists use observations to determine how much stress is building up along fault lines. They use satellite pictures to examine fault lines, and they watch for changes. As the stress increases, scientists know the risk of an earthquake is greater. They are able to warn people that an earthquake might hit in the near future. Seismologists are still unable to predict exactly when an earthquake will happen. But, by studying earthquakes of the past, they become better and better at predicting earthquakes of the future.

TOP TEN WORST EARTHQUAKES

1. **CHILE, EARTHQUAKE OF 1960, MAGNITUDE 9.5**
   This is the world's strongest recorded earthquake. Approximately 4,485 people died or were injured. The earthquake created a tsunami and caused damage as far away as Hawaii, Japan, the Philippines, and the West Coast of the United States.

2. **ALASKA, EARTHQUAKE OF 1964, MAGNITUDE 9.2**
   This earthquake began in Prince William Sound. It lasted more than four minutes and was felt as far south as Oregon and California. Altogether, 131 people died.

3. **NORTHERN SUMATRA, EARTHQUAKE OF 2004, MAGNITUDE 9.1**
   Approximately 228,000 people died in this earthquake and the tsunami it created. The worst destruction was seen in South Asia and East Africa.

4. **JAPAN, EARTHQUAKE AND TSUNAMI OF 2011, MAGNITUDE 9.0**
   This earthquake and the resulting tsunami killed more than 20,000 people. Severe damage occurred at the nuclear power plant in Fukushima, resulting in radioactive leaks into the water, on land, and in the air.

5. **KAMCHATKA, RUSSIA, EARTHQUAKE OF 1952, MAGNITUDE 9.0**
   Most of the destruction caused by this Russian earthquake was from the tsunami it created. Because the earthquake occurred in an area of low population, no lives were lost.

6. **BIO-BIO, CHILE, EARTHQUAKE OF 2010, MAGNITUDE 8.8**
   More than 500 people died in this earthquake and tsunami. It caused tsunami waves as far away as Canada and New Zealand.

7. **ECUADOR, EARTHQUAKE OF 1906, MAGNITUDE 8.8**
   This earthquake created a tsunami that killed between 500 and 1,500 people.

8. **RAT ISLANDS, ALASKA, EARTHQUAKE OF 1965, MAGNITUDE 8.7**
   Because this earthquake occurred in an area of low population, no lives were lost. It caused some damage, as well as flooding from a tsunami.

9. **SUMATRA, EARTHQUAKE OF 2005, MAGNITUDE 8.6**
   More than 1,000 people died in this earthquake and tsunami. The tsunami affected communities as far away as Thailand and the Maldives.

10. **ASSAM-TIBET, EARTHQUAKE OF 1950, MAGNITUDE 8.6**
    Nearly 800 people died in this earthquake, which caused landslides. It also caused a dam to break, killing another 500 people.

GLOSSARY

BOUNDARY: A dividing line.

FAULT LINES: Breaks in Earth's crust.

MAGNITUDE: The intensity of an earthquake represented by a number on a scale.

MELTDOWN: When the core of a nuclear reactor overheats and melts, releasing dangerous radiation into the environment.

PREPAREDNESS: The quality or state of being prepared.

REACTORS: Devices for the controlled production of nuclear energy.

RUPTURE: A breaking or tearing.

SEISMIC: Related to an earthquake or another shaking of the earth.

SEISMOLOGISTS: Scientists who study earthquakes and the movement of waves that go through Earth.

TECTONIC PLATES: Large pieces of Earth's crust that lie under the continents and oceans and cause seismic activity where they meet.

TSUNAMI: A large wave caused by the shaking of an earthquake.

WAVE: The movement of energy through a material.

FURTHER INFORMATION

BOOKS

Griffey, Harriet. *Earthquakes and Other Natural Disasters.* New York: DK Children, 2010.

Mooney, Carla. *Earthquakes.* Minneapolis: Abdo Publishing, 2013.

Simon, Seymour. *Earthquakes.* New York: HarperCollins, 2006.

Than, Ker. *Earthquakes.* New York: Scholastic, 2009.

WEBSITES

http://earthquake.usgs.gov/learn/kids
This website has activities, project ideas, and information about earthquakes.

http://www.weatherwizkids.com/weather-earthquake.htm
This website explains what happens during an earthquake.

INDEX

aftershocks, 15–16
architecture, 36, 42

Bay Bridge, 36

California, 19, 38, 43
Challenger Deep, 20
China, 5, 42

earthquake safety, 35–36, 38, 40–41, 42
epicenter, 20

fault lines, 13, 16, 19, 43
foreshocks, 13, 15
Fukushima Daiichi Nuclear Power Plant, 5–6

human-caused earthquakes, 13, 23–24
hypocenter, 20

Indian Ocean earthquake and tsunami, 6, 30

Japan, 5–6, 7, 8–10, 15, 19, 30

layers of Earth, 8, 9, 23
liquefaction, 33, 38

magnitude, 6, 17, 20, 30, 38, 42
mainshock, 15–16
Mariana Trench, 20
moment magnitude scale, 17

Noda, Yoshihiko, 8–9
nuclear reactors, 7–9

Okhotsk plate, 19
Ortelius, Abraham, 24

P waves, 22, 23
Pacific Ocean, 5, 10, 20, 30
Pacific plate, 19
Pangaea, 33

radiation, 7–8
retrofitting, 36
Richter, Charles, 17
Richter scale, 6, 17, 20
Ring of Fire, 30
rupture distance, 16
rupture front, 15–16

S waves, 22, 23
San Francisco earthquake, 30, 32, 43
sea walls, 6, 7
seismic waves, 10, 17, 20, 23
seismographs, 15
seismologists, 6, 10, 15–17, 30, 33, 35, 42, 43
seismometers, 16, 17
subduction zone, 20
surface waves, 23

tectonic plates, 13, 15–16, 19, 20, 30, 32–33
Tohoku earthquake, 5–6, 9–10, 15, 19, 42
tsunami waves, 7, 10, 28, 29, 36
tsunamis, 6–7, 8–9, 29, 30, 35

warning systems, 6, 16, 35
Wegener, Alfred, 24